NLP and Mindfulness:

A Combined Approach to Wellness

By Rex Morton

Disclaimer

This book is intended to provide information about the fields of Neuro-Linguistic Programming (NLP) and Cognitive Behavioural Therapy (CBT) and their potential integration. While the author has made every effort to ensure that the information was correct at the time of publication, the author does not assume and hereby disclaims any liability to any party for any loss, damage, or disruption caused by errors or omissions, whether such errors or omissions result from negligence, accident, or any other cause.

The contents of this book should not be used as a substitute for professional advice, diagnosis, or treatment. The reader should always consult with a qualified healthcare provider about any mental health concerns or conditions. Never disregard professional psychological or medical advice or delay in seeking it because of something you have read in this book.

The views expressed in this work are solely those of the author and do not necessarily reflect the views of the publisher, and the publisher hereby disclaims any responsibility for them.

The inclusion of websites, links, or references to other resources does not mean that the author or the publisher endorses the information the organization or website may provide or recommendations it might make. Furthermore, the author does not guarantee the accuracy of the information these resources provide.

The use of any information provided in this book is solely at your own risk.

Welcome to "NLP and Mindfulness: A Combined Approach to Wellness." This book is designed to guide you on a transformative journey towards achieving optimal wellness through the powerful combination of Neuro-Linguistic Programming (NLP) and Mindfulness.

Wellness is a state of complete physical, mental, and social well-being, not just the absence of disease. A proactive process involves becoming aware and making choices to lead a healthier and more fulfilling life. In our fast-paced world, stress, anxiety, and the pressure to perform can often lead us to neglect our wellness. However, it is crucial to remember that our health and well-being are the foundations upon which we build our lives.

This book aims to provide you with the tools and techniques to enhance your wellness, using two potent methodologies: NLP and Mindfulness.

NLP, also known as Neuro-Linguistic Programming, is a psychological approach that involves analyzing strategies used by successful individuals and implementing them to achieve a personal goal. The relationship between thoughts, language, and patterns of behavior learned through experience is based on specific outcomes.

On the other hand, mindfulness is a mental state achieved by focusing one's consciousness on the present moment, while quietly recognizing and accepting one's feelings, thoughts and bodily sensations. It is often used as a therapeutic technique to manage stress, anxiety, and depression.

While NLP equips you with the strategies to change your thought patterns and behaviors, Mindfulness allows you to cultivate a state of awareness and presence, enhancing your overall well-being. When combined, these two powerful techniques can significantly improve your mental, emotional, and physical wellness.

In the chapters that follow, we will delve deeper into the concepts of NLP and Mindfulness, explore their benefits, and provide practical techniques for integrating these practices into your daily life. We will also share real-life examples and case studies to illustrate the transformative power of these combined methodologies.

Whether you are a seasoned practitioner or a beginner in the realm of personal development, this book will provide valuable insights and practical tools to enhance your wellness journey.

So, let's embark on this exciting journey towards a healthier,

more balanced, and fulfilling life.

Wellness is a term that has gained significant attention in recent years, but what does it truly mean? In its simplest form, wellness refers to the state of being in good health. However, it is a much broader concept that encompasses several aspects of our lives.

The World Health Organization defines wellness as "a state of complete physical, mental, and social well-being, and not merely the absence of disease or infirmity." This definition emphasizes that wellness is not just about being free from illness but involves a proactive approach to maintaining and improving health.

Importance of Mental and Physical Wellness

Physical wellness involves taking care of our bodies through regular physical activity, a balanced diet, adequate sleep, and routine health check-ups. It is about respecting and caring for our bodies, recognizing that our daily habits and behaviors have a significant impact on our overall health.

On the other hand, mental wellness is about maintaining a healthy mental state. This includes managing stress, expressing emotions in a healthy way, maintaining positive relationships, and practicing mindfulness. Mental wellness is equally as important as physical wellness, as our mental state can significantly impact our physical health and vice versa.

The integration of mental and physical wellness leads to holistic wellness, which is the ultimate goal. Holistic wellness recognizes that our mental and physical health are interconnected and that we must pay attention to both to achieve overall well-being.

Common Barriers to Wellness

While we all strive for wellness, several barriers can hinder our journey. These barriers can be physical, such as lack of time or access to health resources. They can also be psychological, such as stress, anxiety, or lack of motivation.

Societal pressures and expectations can also act as barriers to wellness. In our fast-paced world, we often prioritize work and productivity over our health. We may neglect our physical health due to busy schedules, or ignore our mental health due to stigma and misunderstanding.

Understanding these barriers is the first step towards overcoming them. In the following chapters, we will explore strategies to navigate these obstacles and enhance our wellness using the combined approach of NLP and Mindfulness.

In conclusion, wellness is a holistic concept that involves both our physical and mental health. It is a proactive and conscious process that requires ongoing effort. Despite the barriers we may face, achieving wellness is possible, and the rewards are well worth the effort.

Chapter 2: Introduction to NLP (Neuro-Linguistic Programming)

Neuro-Linguistic Programming, commonly known as NLP, is a powerful approach to communication, personal development, and psychotherapy. It's a technique that modifies brain activity ("neuro") through influencing language ("linguistic") and other forms of communication, allowing a person to "recode" their brain's response to stimuli ("programming") and exhibit new and improved behaviors.

Definition and History of NLP

NLP was developed in the 1970s by Richard Bandler, a mathematician, and John Grinder, a linguist, at the University of California, Santa Cruz. They were interested in understanding how some people excelled in their fields and how they could model this excellence to help others achieve similar success.

Bandler and Grinder studied successful therapists like Fritz Perls, Virginia Satir, and Milton Erickson and identified patterns in their communication and behavior that contributed to their effectiveness. These patterns became the foundation of NLP.

Basic Principles of NLP

NLP operates on several guiding principles or presuppositions. Here are a few key ones:

The Map is Not the Territory: This principle suggests that our perception of reality is not reality itself but our own subjective experience of it. We all have our unique "maps" or models of the world, shaped by our experiences, beliefs, and values.

There is No Failure, Only Feedback: In NLP, there is no such thing as failure, only feedback. If something doesn't work, it's an opportunity to learn, adjust, and try again.

The Mind and Body are Part of the Same System: Our thoughts, emotions, and physical state are interconnected and influence each other. Changes in one area can lead to changes in others.

If One Person Can Do Something, Anyone Can Learn to Do It: This principle is at the heart of NLP's modeling techniques. If one person can achieve something, it's possible to model their strategies and teach them to others.

How NLP Works

NLP works by identifying, understanding, and applying successful strategies. It involves several techniques, including:

Modeling: Observing and replicating the behaviors, beliefs, and strategies of successful individuals.

Anchoring: Associating a specific physical touch or visual cue with a positive mental state, so it can be accessed at will.

Reframing: Changing the way we perceive an event or experience to change its meaning and impact on us.

Swish Patterns: Replacing an undesirable state or behavior with a desirable one.

Meta Model: A set of questions designed to reveal the underlying assumptions behind language.

Through these techniques, NLP can help individuals improve their communication, change limiting beliefs, overcome fears and phobias, manage stress and anxiety, and achieve personal and professional goals.

In the next chapter, we will delve into the world of Mindfulness, another powerful tool for wellness. As we progress, we will explore how NLP and Mindfulness can be combined for a holistic approach to wellness.

Focusing attention on the present moment while consciously identifying and embracing one's feelings, thoughts, and physical sensations leads to the mental state of mindfulness. Due to its multiple advantages for both physical and mental health, it is a technique that has been gaining popularity recently.

Definition and History of Mindfulness

Simple definitions of mindfulness include paying attention in the present moment, on purpose, and without passing judgment. The inventor of the Mindfulness-Based Stress Reduction (MBSR) program, Jon Kabat-Zinn, gave this definition that perfectly captures the core of mindfulness.

The concept of mindfulness has its roots in ancient Buddhist meditation practices, particularly Vipassana, which means "to see things as they really are." However, mindfulness as we know it today has been largely influenced by the work of Kabat-Zinn, who in the late 1970s, adapted these ancient practices to create the MBSR program. This program, designed to help patients deal with pain, stress, and illness, has been widely researched and is used in many medical and psychological interventions today.

Basic Principles of Mindfulness

Mindfulness is based on a few key principles:

Present Moment Awareness: Mindfulness involves bringing one's attention to the experiences occurring in the present moment. It is about being fully engaged in whatever we are doing right now, rather than dwelling in the past or anticipating the future.

Non-Judgmental Observation: Mindfulness encourages observing our thoughts and feelings from a distance, without judging them as good or bad. It's about accepting things as they are without trying to change them.

Acceptance: Mindfulness involves accepting things as they are, rather than how we want them to be. It's about acknowledging and accepting our thoughts, feelings, and sensations without resistance.

Non-Attachment: Mindfulness teaches us to let go of our attachment to thoughts, feelings, and outcomes. It's about understanding the impermanent nature of things and learning to let go.

How Mindfulness Works

Mindfulness works by helping us shift our focus from our thoughts to our sensory experiences. When we're mindful, we're aware of our breath, our body, and our immediate environment. We're fully engaged in the present moment, rather than being lost in our thoughts.

Mindfulness practices often involve meditation, but they can also include other activities like mindful eating, mindful walking, or even mindful dishwashing. The goal is to cultivate a state of mindfulness that we can carry into every aspect of our lives.

Mindfulness helps us to reduce stress, improve focus, manage difficult emotions, and enhance our overall well-being. It allows us to experience life more fully, as we're no longer caught up in our thoughts about the past or the future.

In the next chapter, we will delve deeper into the power of NLP and how it can transform our lives. As we progress, we will explore how NLP and Mindfulness can be combined for a holistic approach to wellness.

Neuro-Linguistic Programming (NLP) is a powerful tool that can bring about significant changes in our lives. It offers a range of benefits, from improving communication skills to overcoming fears and limiting beliefs.

Benefits of NLP

Improved Communication: NLP techniques can help us understand others better and communicate our thoughts and feelings more effectively. This can enhance our personal and professional relationships.

Overcoming Limiting Beliefs: NLP can help us identify and change limiting beliefs that hold us back from achieving our goals.

Managing Stress and Anxiety: NLP offers tools to manage stress and anxiety, promoting mental well-being.

Enhancing Self-Esteem and Confidence: Through NLP, we can boost our self-esteem and confidence, leading to improved performance in various areas of life.

Achieving Personal and Professional Goals: NLP can help us clarify our goals, develop a roadmap to achieve them, and overcome any obstacles along the way.

Hypothetical Case Studies

Case Study 1 - Overcoming Fear of Public Speaking: John, a talented professional, had a fear of public speaking. He would get anxious and stumble over his words during presentations. After learning NLP techniques, he was able to identify and change his negative thought patterns. He used visualization techniques to imagine himself delivering a successful presentation. Over time, John was able to overcome his fear and improve his public speaking skills.

Case Study 2 - Enhancing Self-Esteem: Sarah, a college student, struggled with low self-esteem. She often doubted her abilities and feared failure. Through NLP, Sarah learned to recognize her negative self-talk and replace it with positive affirmations. She also used anchoring techniques to tap into positive states of confidence and self-assuredness. These changes helped Sarah boost her self-esteem and perform better in her studies.

Common Misconceptions about NLP

NLP is a Quick Fix: While NLP can bring about significant changes, it is not a magic pill. It requires consistent practice and application.

NLP is Manipulative: Some people believe that NLP is used to manipulate people. However, the purpose of NLP is to improve communication and understanding, not to manipulate others.

NLP is Only for Therapists or Coaches: While NLP is widely used in therapy and coaching, it is a tool that anyone can learn and benefit from.

In conclusion, NLP is a powerful tool that can bring about significant changes in our lives. It offers a range of benefits, from improving communication skills to overcoming fears and limiting beliefs. However, like any tool, its effectiveness depends on how it is used. With proper understanding and application, NLP can be a valuable asset in our journey towards wellness.

Mindfulness is a simple yet powerful practice that can bring about profound changes in our lives. It offers a range of benefits, from reducing stress to improving mental clarity and emotional well-being.

Benefits of Mindfulness

Reduced Stress and Anxiety: Regular mindfulness practice can help reduce stress and anxiety by helping us stay focused on the present moment rather than getting caught up in worrying thoughts about the past or future.

Improved Mental Clarity and Focus: Mindfulness can enhance our mental clarity and focus by training our mind to stay attentive to the task at hand.

Enhanced Emotional Well-being: By helping us become more aware of our emotions without getting overwhelmed by them, mindfulness can improve our emotional well-being.

Improved Physical Health: Research has shown that mindfulness can have numerous physical health benefits, including improved sleep, lower blood pressure, and even pain relief.

Increased Self-Awareness: Mindfulness helps us become more aware of our thoughts, feelings, and bodily sensations, promoting greater self-understanding and self-acceptance.

Hypothetical Case Studies

Case Study 1 - Managing Stress at Work: Jane, a busy corporate executive, was feeling overwhelmed by stress at work. She started practicing mindfulness meditation for 10 minutes each morning. Over time, she found that she was better able to manage her stress levels, stay focused during meetings, and respond to challenges with greater calm and clarity.

Case Study 2 - Dealing with Chronic Pain: Mike, a middle-aged man suffering from chronic back pain, started attending a Mindfulness-Based Stress Reduction (MBSR) program. Through mindfulness exercises and meditation, he learned to observe his pain without judgment and to recognize the difference between physical pain and his emotional reactions to it. This helped him manage his pain better and improved his quality of life.

Common Misconceptions about Mindfulness

Mindfulness is Just About Relaxation: While mindfulness can help us relax, its primary purpose is to help us become more aware of our present-moment experience, whether it's comfortable or uncomfortable.

Mindfulness is a Religious Practice: While mindfulness has roots in Buddhism, the mindfulness practices used in health and wellness contexts are secular and can be practiced by anyone, regardless of their religious or philosophical beliefs.

Mindfulness Requires a Lot of Time: You can practice mindfulness in just a few minutes a day, and you can incorporate mindfulness into your daily activities, like eating, walking, or washing dishes.

In conclusion, mindfulness is a powerful practice that can bring about significant changes in our lives. It offers a range of benefits, from reducing stress to improving mental clarity and emotional well-being. However, like any practice, it requires regular and consistent practice to reap its benefits. With proper understanding and application, mindfulness can be a valuable asset in our journey towards wellness.

NLP and Mindfulness, while different in their approaches, can complement each other beautifully. When combined, they can enhance the benefits of each other and provide a holistic approach to personal development and wellness.

The Synergy between NLP and Mindfulness

NLP focuses on understanding and changing our thought patterns and behaviors to achieve desired outcomes, while Mindfulness emphasizes being present and accepting our experiences without judgment. When used together, NLP can provide the tools to change unhelpful patterns, and Mindfulness can provide the awareness needed to recognize these patterns in the first place.

How NLP Can Enhance Mindfulness Practices

Creating a Mindful State: NLP techniques can be used to create a state of mindfulness. For example, the NLP technique of anchoring can be used to trigger a mindful state at will.

Enhancing Focus: NLP techniques can help enhance the focus that is essential in mindfulness practices. Techniques such as the

'Visual-Kinesthetic Dissociation' can help individuals manage distracting thoughts and stay focused on the present moment.

Dealing with Resistance: Sometimes, individuals may resist mindfulness practices due to underlying fears or beliefs. NLP can help address these barriers and make it easier for individuals to embrace mindfulness.

How Mindfulness Can Enhance NLP Techniques

Increasing Self-Awareness: Mindfulness, by enhancing self-awareness, can make NLP techniques more effective. When we are more aware of our thoughts, feelings, and behaviors, we can use NLP techniques more effectively to change unhelpful patterns.

Enhancing Emotional Regulation: Mindfulness can enhance the effectiveness of NLP techniques used for emotional regulation. By helping us stay present with our emotions, mindfulness can enhance the effectiveness of NLP techniques like 'Swish' or 'Reframing' that are used for managing emotions.

Deepening Understanding of Self and Others: Mindfulness can enhance NLP techniques used for understanding self and others. By promoting a non-judgmental, present-moment awareness, mindfulness can deepen the insights gained from NLP techniques like 'Perceptual Positions'.

Examples of Combining NLP and Mindfulness

Example 1 - Managing Stress: An individual could use mindfulness to become aware of the physical sensations and thoughts associated with stress. Then, they could use NLP techniques to change their response to these stress triggers.

Example 2 - Enhancing Communication: An individual could use mindfulness to become more aware of their own communication patterns and the reactions of others. They could then use NLP techniques to improve their communication skills.

Example 3 - Overcoming Limiting Beliefs: An individual could use mindfulness to become aware of limiting beliefs that hold them back. They could then use NLP techniques to challenge and change these beliefs.

In conclusion, NLP and Mindfulness, when combined, can provide a powerful approach to personal development and wellness. By enhancing self-awareness, focus, and emotional regulation, and by providing tools to change unhelpful patterns, this combined approach can help individuals achieve their wellness goals.

Integrating NLP and Mindfulness into daily life can have profound effects on various aspects of our lives, including stress management, relationships, and productivity. Here are some practical techniques and exercises for doing so.

Techniques and Exercises for Integrating NLP and Mindfulness into Daily Life

Mindful Anchoring: Use the NLP technique of anchoring to create a trigger for a mindful state. For example, each time you touch your thumb and forefinger together, take a moment to focus on your breath and bring your attention to the present moment.

Visual-Kinesthetic Dissociation for Stress Management: When you notice yourself getting stressed, use this NLP technique to 'step out' of the stressful situation and view it from a third-person perspective. Combine this with mindfulness by observing your thoughts and feelings without judgment.

Mindful Reframing: Use the NLP technique of reframing to change your perspective on a challenging situation. Practice mindfulness as you do this, staying present with your feelings and observing how they change as you shift your perspective.

How to Use NLP and Mindfulness for Stress Management, Improving Relationships, Enhancing Productivity, etc.

Stress Management: Use mindfulness to become aware of your stress triggers and physical responses to stress. Then, use NLP techniques like reframing or anchoring to change your response to these triggers.

Example: If you notice that you're feeling stressed before a big presentation, you could use mindfulness to observe your thoughts and physical sensations. Then, you could use an NLP anchoring technique to trigger a state of calm and confidence.

Improving Relationships: Use mindfulness to become more aware of your own communication patterns and the reactions of others. Then, use NLP techniques to improve your communication skills.

Example: If you notice that you often interrupt others during conversations, you could use mindfulness to become more aware of this habit. Then, you could use NLP techniques to practice active listening and improve your communication skills.

Enhancing Productivity: Use mindfulness to stay focused on the task at hand and avoid distractions. Use NLP techniques to set clear goals and create a roadmap for achieving them.

Example: If you're working on a big project, you could use mindfulness to stay focused and present with the task at hand. You could use NLP goal-setting techniques to create a clear plan for the project and stay motivated.

In conclusion, integrating NLP and Mindfulness into daily life can have profound effects on various aspects of our lives. By enhancing self-awareness, focus, and emotional regulation, and by providing tools to change unhelpful patterns, these practices can help us manage stress, improve relationships, enhance productivity, and achieve our wellness goals.

Chapter 8: Overcoming Challenges in Practicing NLP and Mindfulness

While the benefits of NLP and Mindfulness are numerous, practicing them consistently can sometimes be challenging. Here are some common challenges and tips on how to overcome them.

Common Challenges and How to Overcome Them

Finding Time: One of the most common challenges is finding time to practice NLP and Mindfulness regularly. To overcome this, try to integrate these practices into your daily routine. For example, practice mindfulness while commuting or doing household chores. For NLP, you can practice techniques like reframing or anchoring in response to daily events.

Staying Focused: It can be challenging to stay focused during mindfulness practice or when applying NLP techniques. Remember that it's normal for the mind to wander. When you notice this happening, gently bring your attention back to the present moment or the NLP technique you're practicing.

Dealing with Uncomfortable Emotions: Both NLP and Mindfulness can bring up uncomfortable emotions. It's important to approach these emotions with kindness and curiosity rather than trying to push them away. If certain emotions become overwhelming, consider seeking support from a mental health professional.

Tips for Staying Motivated

Set Clear Goals: Having clear goals can help you stay motivated. Your goals could be related to stress management, improving relationships, or enhancing productivity.

Practice Regularly: Like any skill, NLP and Mindfulness improve with regular practice. Try to set aside some time each day for these practices, even if it's just a few minutes.

Be Patient with Yourself: Change takes time. Be patient with yourself and celebrate small victories along the way.

How to Make NLP and Mindfulness a Habit

Start Small: If you're new to NLP and Mindfulness, start with small, manageable practices. For example, you could start with just 5 minutes of mindfulness meditation per day or one simple NLP technique.

Integrate into Daily Life: Try to integrate NLP and Mindfulness into your daily life. Practice mindfulness during routine activities like eating or walking. Apply NLP techniques in response to daily events.

Create a Supportive Environment: Create an environment that supports your practice. This could include setting a regular time and place for practice, having a meditation cushion or chair, or surrounding yourself with supportive people.

Examples of Overcoming Challenges

Example 1 - Finding Time: John, a busy professional, found it hard to find time for practice. He started practicing mindfulness during his daily commute and found that this not only helped him find time for practice but also made his commute more enjoyable.

Example 2 - Staying Focused: Maria found it hard to stay focused during mindfulness practice. She started using a guided meditation app, which helped her stay focused and made her practice more enjoyable.

Example 3 - Making it a Habit: Mike wanted to make NLP and Mindfulness a habit. He started by setting a goal of practicing for

5 minutes each day. Over time, he gradually increased this time, and these practices became a regular part of his daily routine.

The practice of NLP and mindfulness can be difficult, but with perseverance, the correct techniques, and patience, these difficulties can be overcome. By integrating these practices into daily life, setting clear goals, and creating a supportive environment, you can make NLP and Mindfulness a regular part of your life and reap their many benefits.

To illustrate the practical application of NLP and Mindfulness, let's look at some hypothetical case studies of individuals who have successfully used these techniques for wellness.

Case Study 1: Overcoming Anxiety with NLP and Mindfulness

Sarah, a software engineer, was struggling with anxiety related to her job. She often found herself worrying about deadlines and her performance, which was affecting her sleep and overall wellbeing.

Sarah started practicing mindfulness meditation for 10 minutes each day. This helped her become more aware of her anxious thoughts without getting caught up in them. She also used the NLP technique of reframing to change her perspective on her job and her performance. Instead of viewing her job as a source of stress, she started seeing it as an opportunity to learn and grow.

Over time, Sarah noticed a significant reduction in her anxiety levels. She was sleeping better, felt more relaxed at work, and even received positive feedback from her boss about her improved performance.

Case Study 2: Improving Relationships with NLP and Mindfulness

David, a sales manager, was having difficulty communicating with his team. He often found himself getting frustrated and impatient, which was affecting his relationships with his team members.

David started practicing mindfulness to become more aware of his emotions and reactions. He also used NLP techniques to improve his communication skills. For example, he used the technique of mirroring to better understand his team members and communicate more effectively with them.

Over time, David noticed a significant improvement in his relationships with his team members. He was able to communicate more effectively, his team's performance improved, and the overall atmosphere in his team became more positive.

Case Study 3: Enhancing Productivity with NLP and Mindfulness

Emma, a freelance writer, was struggling with procrastination. She often found herself distracted and had difficulty staying focused on her work.

Emma started practicing mindfulness to stay focused on the task at hand and avoid distractions. She also used NLP techniques to set clear goals and create a roadmap for achieving them. For example, she used the technique of future pacing to visualize her success and stay motivated.

Over time, Emma noticed a significant improvement in her productivity. She was able to stay focused on her work, meet her deadlines, and even found more enjoyment in her writing.

In conclusion, these case studies illustrate how NLP and Mindfulness can be used to overcome challenges and enhance wellness. Whether it's managing anxiety, improving relationships, or enhancing productivity, these techniques can provide effective tools for personal development and wellbeing.

As we reach the end of this book, let's take a moment to recap what we've learned and look forward to the journey ahead.

We started by exploring the concept of wellness, understanding its importance, and recognizing the common barriers that often stand in our way. We then delved into the world of Neuro-Linguistic Programming (NLP) and Mindfulness, understanding their principles, how they work, and the power they hold in transforming our lives.

Through various chapters, we discovered the synergy between NLP and Mindfulness and how they can be combined for a more holistic approach to wellness. We learned practical techniques and exercises for integrating these practices into our daily lives, and we explored how to overcome common challenges that might arise along the way.

Through hypothetical case studies, we saw how individuals like Sarah, David, and Emma successfully used NLP and Mindfulness to overcome anxiety, improve relationships, and enhance productivity. Their stories serve as inspiration for what is possible when we commit to this path.

As you close this book, remember that the journey to wellness is a personal one, and it's not always a straight path. There will be challenges and obstacles, but with the tools and techniques you've learned in this book, you are well-equipped to navigate them.

Remember, the practices of NLP and Mindfulness are not one-time solutions but ongoing practices. They are like muscles that grow stronger with regular exercise. So, keep practicing, stay patient with yourself, and celebrate your progress along the way.

Your journey to wellness is a journey of self-discovery, growth, and transformation. It's a journey worth embarking on. As you continue on this path, remember to be kind to yourself, stay open to new experiences, and trust in your ability to create positive change in your life.

Thank you for taking this journey with us through the pages of this book. We hope it has provided you with valuable insights and practical tools for your wellness journey. Remember, the journey doesn't end here. It's just the beginning. Keep exploring, keep learning, and keep growing. Your journey to wellness is just getting started.

Rex Morton is a renowned author and researcher in the United Kingdom with a passionate interest in the human mind, specifically in Cognitive Behavioural Therapy (CBT) and Neuro-Linguistic Programming (NLP).

Morton has spent a considerable portion of his professional life diving deep into the theories and principles that form the backbone of these two compelling fields. His fascination with NLP led him to complete an extensive certification program, solidifying his understanding of this innovative approach to understanding human behaviour.

Although Morton does not have clinical experience, his intense curiosity and dedication to studying these subjects have made him a respected figure in the field. He has thoroughly researched the integration of NLP techniques into CBT, offering fresh perspectives and insights into how these two methodologies can complement each other to enhance understanding of human cognition and behaviour.

As an author, Morton has successfully communicated his knowledge and passion to a broader audience, making complex psychological theories accessible to professionals and interested laypersons. His writing is characterized by a clear, engaging style and a focus on the practical application of theories, making them relevant to everyday life.

In his personal life, Morton is an ardent lover of the natural world, often spending his free time exploring the British countryside. His passion for landscape photography allows him to capture and share the beauty of these excursions. Despite his accomplishments, Morton is known for his humility and eagerness to continue learning. His work continues to inspire those interested in the intricate workings of the human mind and the exciting possibilities presented by the integration of NLP and CBT.

If you've found the content of this book enlightening and wish to continue your journey of understanding the human mind, I warmly invite you to visit my website at www.rexmorton.com. The website serves as a hub of knowledge where I share my latest findings, thoughts, and insights on the integration of NLP and CBT.

I also encourage you to subscribe to the newsletter available on the website. By subscribing, you'll receive regular updates on a range of topics, from detailed discussions on specific NLP techniques and their application in CBT, to the latest research in the field.

The newsletter is also the first place I'll share news of upcoming releases. Whether it's the announcement of a new book, the launch of an online course, newsletter subscribers will be the first to know. This is a great opportunity to continue learning directly from me, deepening your understanding of NLP and CBT, and enhancing your skills in applying these techniques in your own life or professional practice.

I'm looking forward to sharing this journey with you.